HIDDEN HISTORIES

of Swansea and Gower

Gary Gregor

The Gower Society
2014

Published by The Gower Society, Swansea

ISBN 978-0-902767-20-1

Printed in Wales by
Dinefwr Press
Rawlings Road, Llandybie,
Carmarthenshire, SA18 3YD

ACKNOWLEDGEMENTS

Thanks to Malcolm and Ruth Ridge for their editing and help with illustrations.

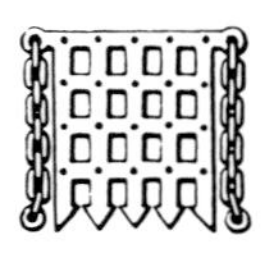

For further information on The Gower Society and its publications, go to *www.thegowersociety.org.uk*

CONTENTS

Oxwich Castle
(Ernest Morgan)

Oxwich Castle
(Ernest Morgan)

THE AFFRAY AT OXWICH CASTLE

Slain by a stone

Nearly five hundred years ago London's Court of Star Chamber became involved in administering justice after a killing in rural Gower.

The Swansea suburb of Manselton and the Gower hamlet of Mansel-field take their names from the Mansel family, after whom streets in Swansea, Gowerton, and other places are named. In the early 1500s Sir Rice Mansel built Oxwich castle, hidden among the trees above Oxwich Bay, as a fortified Tudor manor house – with his initials and coat of arms carved in stone above the gateway. It was near that gateway that a member of the Mansel family died in an altercation on Boxing Day in 1557.

For centuries the Gower coast was hazardous for shipping in bad weather conditions, and in the storms of that late December a French ship ran aground. Since England was at war with France, local people had no compunction about seizing the cargo and detaining the surviving seamen. But when news of the wreck reached Swansea, Sir George Herbert, who was steward of the Earl of Worcester, lord of Gower, and no friend of the Mansels, hurried to Oxwich with a group of armed men, determined to recover the booty.

Having ransacked several cottages in the village to retrieve goods taken from the shipwreck, they moved on to the castle. Sir Rice Mansel was away, but his son Edward stood up to the demands of Sir George, while his aunt Lady Anne Mansel from Llanddewi endeavoured to calm the situation. As the group was reluctantly withdrawing, one of Sir George's men flung a stone: it struck Lady Anne Mansel, and caused her death.

The Court of Star Chamber (so called because of the star pattern painted on the ceiling) had been established at the Palace of Westminster to enforce the law against prominent people whose influence might hinder an ordinary court from convicting them. Sir George and his men were summoned before the court, and justice administered by fines, imprison-ment, and the return of goods seized.

Even rural Gower was not beyond the reach of English law in Tudor times.

Bust of Edgar Evans by Philip Chatfield
in Swansea Museum

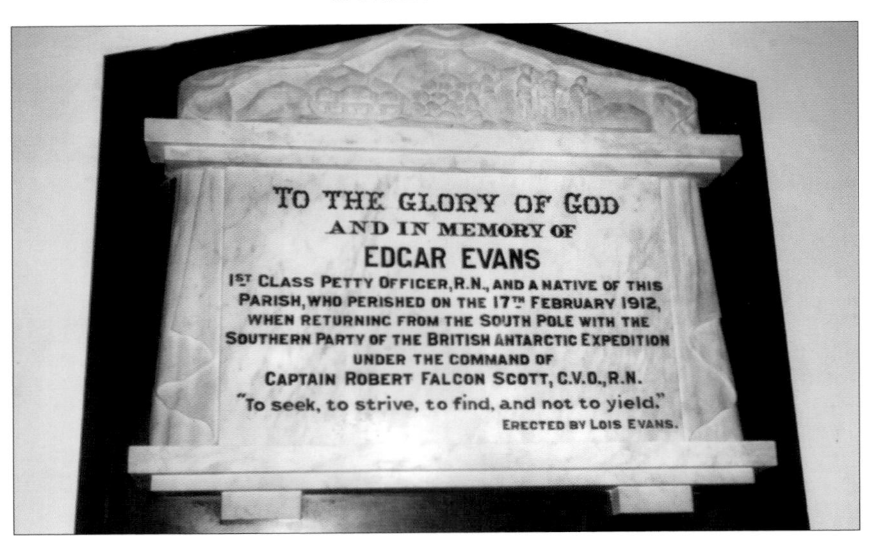

Memorial plaque in Rhossili Church

ANTARCTIC HERO

From the Castle to the ends of the earth

Varsity Swansea stands on the corner where Wind Street joins St Mary's Street. This 1908 building in Edwardian Baroque style used to be the Midland Bank (and more recently HSBC), before renovation and change of use. It has no direct connection with Captain Scott's last expedition to Antarctica, but it replaced a building on that site that did. This was the Castle Hotel, often patronised by captains of the copper ore barques that used to sail across the Atlantic Ocean, before a hazardous passage around Cape Horn, to collect copper ore from South American countries such as Chile, to bring back to the copper works that proliferated in the Lower Swansea Valley.

In 1891, after leaving St Helen's School in Vincent Street, a young lad from Rhossili named Edgar Evans spent a year working at the Castle Hotel, until at the age of sixteen he was old enough to join the Royal Navy. One surmises that in hearing those sea captains speak of their experiences, Edgar would have been further motivated to join the Navy. After he did so and had demonstrated his ability as a petty officer, Edgar was selected for both of Captain Scott's expeditions to Antarctica, first in the *Discovery*, and then in the *Terra Nova*, which sailed from Cardiff in 1910. January 2012 marked the centenary of when five members of that expedition, including Captain Scott and Edgar Evans, reached the South Pole, though all perished on the return journey. A bust of Edgar is in Swansea Museum, his old school St Helen's displays a photo of him, inside Rhossili church a plaque hangs in his memory, and the Royal Mail premises on the Enterprise Zone display H. A. Chapman's photo at the time of his wedding. This is because during his time at school Edgar had worked part-time as a telegraph messenger boy, based at the Head Post Office that used to stand in front of Swansea castle – and nearly opposite what was the Castle Hotel.

Lady Barham, from a painting by Angelica Kauffman

Mount Pisgah, Parkmill (1822)

Bethel, Penclawdd (1816)

Immanuel, Pilton Green (1821)

Bethesda, Burry Green (1814)

Trinity, Cheriton (1816)

Paraclete, Newton (1818)

LADY BARHAM

When the light from Fairy Hill lit up Gower

What links Gower's oldest chapel with the peninsula's five-star hotel? Surfers driving to Llangennith may not notice the white chapel on their right as they hurry through Burry Green. It is the oldest chapel in Gower still in regular use, with morning and evening meetings each Sunday, and celebrated its two-hundredth anniversary in 2013. Unusually the entrance to the balcony inside is via an outside stairway. Bethesda chapel was the first of six chapels built over a ten-year period by Diana, Lady Barham, who lived at Fairy Hill – now a five-star hotel.

Diana Middleton (no relation to the Duchess of Cambridge) was born to parents involved in the campaign to abolish the slave trade – her home, Barham Court in Teston, Kent, was where the meetings took place with William Wilberforce and Thomas Clarkson to plan the campaign. Her father was First Lord of the Admiralty, created Baron Barham after the battle of Trafalgar. When aged seventeen, Diana married Sir Gerard Noel, an eccentric landowner from Rutland, who it seems did not share her Christian faith. They had a large family, but after her father's death in 1812 she became financially independent when inheriting the title Lady Barham.

Lady Barham used her inheritance to erect chapels and schoolrooms in Gower, where there was little provision for nonconformists, who would not use the Church of England liturgy in worship. Moving to Fairy Hill when she was aged fifty-one, Lady Barham built chapels (used on weekdays as schoolrooms) at Burry Green, Penclawdd, Cheriton, Newton, Pilton Green (now a private home) and at Parkmill.

In the days before any National Health Service she often paid medical expenses for the villagers. When a young girl presented her with yet another bill she asked 'What did you people do before I came?' and received the reply 'Please, ma'am, we died'. The bill was paid forthwith.

Diana, Lady Barham, died aged sixty-one, and is remembered on a plaque behind the pulpit in Burry Green chapel, where her picture hangs in the vestry.

The fire at the Church of the Compañía de Jesús

After the fire

THE BELLS OF SANTIAGO

Chile to Mumbles to Chile

The Bells in Oystermouth Church porch before their return to Santiago

The churches of Bishopston and Llangennith contain one or more bells cast in the early eighteenth century by the bell-founder David Davies of Oystermouth. So you might expect that any bells at All Saints church in Mumbles would be cast by the same bell-founder, but that is not the case. The four bells dating from 1753 which for over 150 years were housed at All Saints church were cast much further afield – in north-eastern Spain. Before coming to Oystermouth they used to hang in the Jesuit cathedral in Santiago, Chile, until they crashed to the ground during a disastrous fire in 1863. During the final night of a month-long festival in honour of the Virgin Mary, the packed Church de la Compañía de Jesús, full of incense, oil lights, liquid gas lights and wax candles, was burned down, and 2,500 persons – mainly women and children – lost their lives. Subsequently the remaining walls of the church were razed to the ground, and the site was transformed into a garden.

This was at the height of the copper ore trade between Swansea and Chile. Graham Vivian of Clyne Castle and of Vivian & Sons arranged for the four bells, which were sold as scrap, to be taken overland to Valparaiso, and shipped by a copper barque to Mumbles. They were hung in the tower of All Saints church until 1964, when for reasons of safety they were taken down and displayed in the church porch.

After the Chilean filmmaker Pedro Pablo Cabrera discovered the source of the bells, the Parochial Church Council agreed unanimously to a request from the Chilean ambassador for their return. With the aid of a Royal Navy ship, three bells were transported to Chile in September 2010, to be the focus of a memorial for the 150th anniversary of the catastrophe. Only the smallest bell remains at All Saints church – a reminder of that tragedy, and of the links between Swansea and Chile, and between Oystermouth and Santiago.

Evening Post

LATE TOWN FINAL

...re remains, discovered by cave explorers, those of brunette Mamie Stuart?

SKELETON FOUND IN A GOWER MINE-SHAFT

Disappearance of woman in 1919

Evening Post, 6th November 1961

George Shotton and Mamie Stuart

THE BRANDY COVE SKELETON

Grisly secret uncovered

Just west of Caswell is the inlet of Brandy Cove, with a raised beach that is only exposed at low tide. Originally called Hareslade, it was re-named through its usage for smuggling during the 18th century. On Sunday, 5th November 1961, three cavers who were exploring an abandoned lead mine made the grisly discovery of a human skull. They then found a dismembered human skeleton, along with other items including a wedding and engagement ring. When the police looked at files of missing persons they found a file on 26-year-old Mamie Stuart who had disappeared 42 years earlier, and after superimposing her photo onto a photograph of the skull they suspected that the body was hers.

Mamie had been a chorus girl in pantomimes in Cardiff and Swansea, before, in 1918, she married Cardiff marine surveyor George Shotton, though unaware that he was already married – and the father of a child. They rented Craig Eithin, a cottage in Caswell Bay, but suspicions were aroused when her parents were unable to contact Mamie. Shotton reported her missing in late 1919, but then a suitcase was found at Swansea's Grosvenor Hotel containing some of Mamie's possessions. Shotton was brought to trial, but with no body the charge was not murder but bigamy, for which he was sentenced to 18 months' hard labour. Subsequently it is believed he joined the merchant navy.

At the 1962 coroner's inquest in Gowerton, the three potholers gave evidence, as did an elderly man who recalled that when he was a young postman he saw Shotton outside Craig Eithin, struggling to load a sack into his van. The inquest jury decided the skeleton was that of Mamie Stuart and took the unusual step of naming the murderer – George Shotton.

But if he was the murderer it was too late to bring him to justice, for he had died three years earlier, aged 78, penniless in Bristol.

Alcock and Brown statue at Heathrow Airport

Take-off, 1919

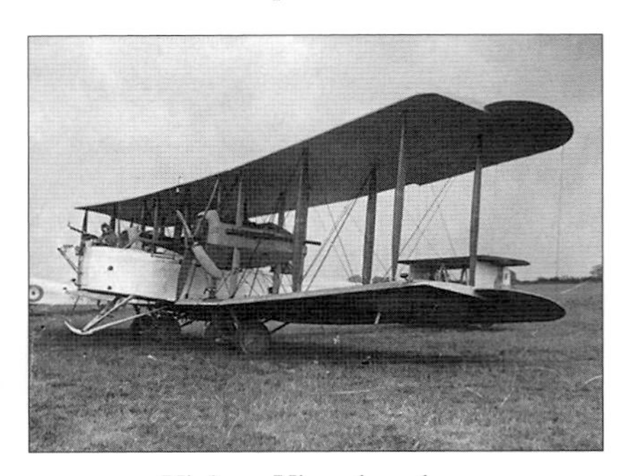

Vickers Vimy bomber

SIR ARTHUR WHITTEN BROWN

First to fly the Atlantic

A plaque in the wall of Overland Road in Langland states that the aviator Sir Arthur Whitten Brown lived in Overland Court. The names of Alcock and Brown became famous when in June 1919 they flew in a modified Vickers Vimy bomber from Newfoundland to Ireland, achieving the first non-stop transatlantic flight. It took them sixteen hours (fourteen and a half of which were over the north Atlantic) to cover 1,890 miles at an average speed of 115 mph. They encountered fog, snow, ice, and much bad visibility; several times Brown, who was the navigator, had to climb out on the wings to remove ice from the engine air intakes. For achieving the first transatlantic flight they received a £10,000 prize (worth £450,000 today) put up by the *Daily Mail*, and a knighthood from King George V at Windsor Castle.

Six months later John Alcock, who was pilot on that epic flight, was killed while flying a new Vickers Viking amphibian to the Paris airshow.

Born to American parents in Glasgow, Brown's career was in engineering. During the First World War his plane was twice shot down and he was a prisoner of war in Germany.

He subsequently worked for Metropolitan-Vickers, being appointed their chief representative in the Swansea area in 1923. One of the propellers from the Vickers Vimy hung for many years on the wall of his Wind Street office before he presented it to the RAF College Cranwell.

At the time of the 1926 General Strike he served as a special constable with the County Borough of Swansea Police. Two years later he went to Burry Port to congratulate Amelia Earhart after her 1928 transatlantic flight.

But the death of his only son, in a 1944 aircraft crash in Holland while serving with the RAF, affected him deeply. Sir Arthur Whitten Brown died in 1948 from an accidental overdose of sleeping tablets aged 62, and is buried in Buckinghamshire.

The statue of Alcock and Brown at Heathrow airport was unveiled in 1954, and now stands outside the visitor centre.

Brunel's Landore viaduct, *London Illustrated News*, 29th June 1850

ISAMBARD KINGDOM BRUNEL

A landmark talent

Many people who go to the Liberty Stadium to watch the Ospreys or to see Premier League football might hardly notice the Landore viaduct, which has been a feature nearby for over 160 years. It is a link with the great Victorian engineer Isambard Kingdom Brunel, engineer of the Great Western Railway.

Major examples of Brunel's work are in Bristol, like the SS *Great Britain* and the Clifton Suspension Bridge, or in Devon, like the bridge over the river Tamar at Saltash, but the Landore viaduct is also a fine example of Brunel's genius. Built from 1847 to 1850 to enable the South Wales Railway to cross the canal and the river Tawe to reach Swansea, Brunel's longest viaduct was originally 1,788 feet (a third of a mile) long, with thirty-seven spans, built of Canadian pitch pine. Forty years later its length was substantially reduced by building up an embankment on the eastern side of the valley with slag from the nearby Hafod copper works, and replacing many original timber piers with masonry. But four masonry piers near Neath Road, each pierced with two arches, are part of Brunel's original design.

Elsewhere in this area Brunel designed the four 'flying arches' in Llansamlet to hold back the cutting through which the railway line passes, and at Loughor was his only surviving wooden railway bridge – others have been rebuilt in masonry.

Brunel travelled on the first train from Chepstow to the new terminus station in Swansea's High Street on 18th June 1850, to attend the celebratory banquet held in a marquee on the area where the South Dock was later excavated – now the Marina. He was seated among the principal guests like J. H. Vivian, John Dillwyn Llewelyn and C. R. M. Talbot. The *Cambrian* reported that Brunel's short speech was well received, and that he sat down amid protracted cheering.

Though the original Brunel statue was stolen from Neyland (a replacement now stands on the plinth), Swansea Museum's Cabinet of Curiosities has a model of his Landore viaduct, as it originally looked, still on view.

Rebecca Rioters, *Wikipedia*

A typical Tollhouse, *Wikipedia*

THE CARTERSFORD TOLLGATE MURDER

Murderer transported

In the early nineteenth century in north Gower a stone bridge was erected at Cartersford, between the commons of Fairwood and Pengwern, and a tollgate installed. From 1839, in protest against exorbitant tolls being charged on turnpike roads, tollgates were liable to be attacked by agricultural workers. In what was called the Rebecca Riots men wore women's clothing and were known as Merched Beca (Rebecca's Daughters) – taking the name from a verse in the book of Genesis. There was a major incident near Pontardulais, when nearly two hundred men attacked the Bolgoed tollgate. Many convicted rioters were transported to the colonies, as also happened after an incident at Cartersford in 1845.

Late on the night of 4th January William Eynon, aged in his seventies, was roused by his wife in response to calls to open the Cartersford tollgate. Eynon remonstrated with two men that since they had no horse or wagon they could have gone around the side of the gate without needing to disturb him. The ensuing argument ended with Eynon lying dead on the ground.

At the Assize Court in May, Christopher Batcock of Llanrhidian received twelve months imprisonment for striking William Eynon with a stone, while John Harris was sentenced to seven years transportation – for stabbing Eynon three times.

Transportation to the American colonies had ceased with the War of Independence, so convicts were sent further afield. From 1787 Australia became the major destination – at least for those who managed to survive the four- to six-month passage. In 1803 Tasmania (known then as Van Diemen's Land) was first settled as a penal colony, and since Queensland's Moreton Bay Settlement had closed in 1831, Harris's destination in 1845 may well have been Tasmania.

Transportation from Britain to the colonies ended with the Penal Servitude Act of 1857, though John Harris had little cause for complaint – if he had not been transported then his crime merited his being hanged in Swansea jail.

Pennard Castle

Pennard Castle, J."Warwick" Smith, 1795

THE CASTLE ON THE GREEN

Golf Club's historic landmark

Pennard castle is hardly 'hidden history', being visible from many parts of Gower, and it has been depicted as early as 1741 on a print by Samuel and Nathaniel Buck. Yet less obvious is the fact that it is not owned by Cadw or the National Trust, but by Pennard Golf Club.

This was founded in 1896, when twenty people were given permission by Thomas Penrice of Kilvrough to play golf on Pennard burrows. They initially had a 9 hole course, until in 1908 James Braid, a five times Open champion, was engaged to design an 18 hole course. After the First World War, when the Kilvrough estate had to be broken up in order to pay death duties, Pennard burrows was purchased by the Golf Club. In 1923 the water tower was built of reinforced concrete, and though now disused it remains a prominent landmark from many areas of the peninsula.

The stone Pennard castle was probably built in the late thirteenth century, possibly replacing a wooden structure, but it became inundated by sand when the south coast of Glamorgan (especially around Kenfig) experienced tsunami-like sandstorms in the fourteenth century. An old legend seeks to explain this by suggesting that the 'verry-folks', the fairies of Gower, called down the sandstorm as judgement on the Lord of the castle for harshly dispersing their dancing and music-making on the day of his daughter's wedding!

Though the castle's appearance has not been enhanced by some concrete strengthening of the structure in the 1960s, it is viewed at its best from the north, where the curtain wall is fairly intact, and a stroll from Pennard school across the burrows is well rewarded by the superb views from the ruins.

The castle's former owners include the tyrannical Hugh le Despenser, Lord of Glamorgan during the reign of Edward II. But since 1920 it has had a much more benevolent owner – Pennard Golf Club.

The *City of Bristol* in Rhossili Bay

CITY OF BRISTOL SHIPWRECKED

Steamer runs aground at Llangennith

The ribs of *Helvetia*, the Norwegian barque that ran aground with no loss of life in 1887, are clearly visible protruding through the sand on Rhossili beach. But nearer Burry Holms are the remains of another shipwreck, visible only for a few days each year at the spring tides, when the sea is out to its furthest extent at low tide. On those days part of the engines of *City of Bristol*, a paddle steamer that not only ran aground but also broke up with fatal consequences, can be seen.

Built in Hotwell's Yard in Bristol in 1827, this 210-ton paddle-steamer sailed from Waterford in Ireland on 17 November 1840, with seven passengers and a cargo that included 15 cattle and 280 pigs, transported in open pens on the deck.

Conditions became stormy, visibility deteriorated, and as darkness fell the vessel ran aground in Rhossili bay. Any hopes of floating off at high tide faded when the vessel turned broadside to the pounding seas, and she was further de-stabilised as the terrified pigs rushed from side to side.

Villagers from Llangennith came onto the beach and could hear the cries for help, but in the darkness and with such rough seas no boat could be launched to assist. Around midnight the paddle-steamer broke up, for the following morning revealed a beach littered with debris, bodies and carcasses. Of twenty-nine persons on board, just two members of the crew survived. Inquests were held in the King's Head, Llangennith, sections of the wreckage were auctioned, and carcasses that had been washed ashore were sold by the local agent for Lloyds underwriters. Seventy-two pigs and four cattle which had survived were kept at Cwm Ivy farm until sold.

The shipwreck led to a light vessel being positioned at the western end of the Helwick sandbank, and a lighthouse, initially supported on wooden piles, being erected at Whiteford Point. Now each year the spring tides enable some remains of the *City of Bristol* to be glimpsed just north of Diles Lake on Rhossili beach.

Amy Dillwyn

Memorial plaque

Election Poster 1907

AMY DILLWYN

A remarkable woman

On the seafront adjacent to the West Cross Hotel, just across the road from Tŷ Glyn (now Mumbles Nursing Home), a blue plaque honours the memory of Amy Dillwyn. She was the grand-daughter of Lewis Weston Dillwyn of Sketty Hall, who owned the Cambrian Pottery, and the daughter of Lewis Llewelyn Dillwyn, Liberal MP for Swansea District, and the niece of pioneer photographer John Dillwyn Llewelyn of Penllergare.

Born in 1845 at what used to be Parkwern in Sketty (later to become the nurses' training school), Amy grew up at Hendrefoilan House in Killay, and was presented at court to Queen Victoria. This privileged upbringing did not make her immune from tragedy, for when her fiancé Llewellyn Thomas died of smallpox she was expected to settle for a life of 'quiet spinsterhood and good works'. She began writing novels – her first *The Rebecca Rioter* is set in the Killay area – and reviewing books – her review of *Treasure Island* for *The Spectator* brought its author Robert Louis Stevenson to general notice.

But her father's death in 1892 meant that the 47-year-old Amy had to move from Hendrefoilan House, for she was left the Llansamlet Spelter Works, which was deeply in debt. She moved into lodgings in Tŷ Glyn in West Cross, and took over the zinc factory (in days when for a woman to run such an enterprise was unthinkable), travelling daily to the office in Cambrian Place. She was responsible for the livelihood of a hundred men, at a time when many of them, but not she, had the vote. Aided by a good manager Amy turned the business around into a profitable enterprise.

Amy Dillwyn was able to purchase Tŷ Glyn, and became a benefactor of several Swansea institutions, such as The Infirmary, the Ragged School and the YMCA. When this somewhat eccentric but courageous character, a water polo player and cigar smoker, died in 1935 aged ninety, her ashes were interred in the Dillwyn grave in St Paul's, Sketty. The seafront plaque is inscribed 'To honour the memory of the first woman industrialist'.

Self Portrait, *c.*1853
(Courtesy Richard Morris)

Orchid House 1846. Watercolour by George Delamotte
(Courtesy Richard Morris)

The Round Room at Penllergare. Watercolour by a member of the family
(Courtesy Richard Morris)

JOHN DILLWYN LLEWELYN

Penrice to Penllergare

Inside St Andrew's church in Penrice on 18th June 1833 occurred what in Gower terms might be called 'the wedding of the decade', if not of the century, when John Dillwyn married Emma Talbot. She was the youngest daughter of Thomas Mansel Talbot, who had had the mansion Penrice Castle built in the 1770s to a design by Anthony Keck (designer also of Prince Charles' Gloucestershire home Highgrove). John Dillwyn was the elder son of Lewis Weston Dillwyn, and brother of Lewis Llewelyn Dillwyn, later of Hendrefoilan House. The marriage of John and Emma was to last nearly half a century.

When he attained the age of 21, John Dillwyn had adopted the additional surname 'Llewelyn' as a condition of inheriting the estate of Penllergare. A pioneer photographer, John Dillwyn Llewelyn was linked by his marriage to Emma's cousin of Lacock Abbey, W. H. Fox Talbot, who patented the calotype process of photography. Also present at that Penrice wedding was Rev. Calvert Richard Jones, whose daguerrotype of Margam Castle from 1841 is the earliest photograph taken in Wales: it is in the National Library of Wales in Aberystwyth. Emma Talbot's wedding dress is in Swansea Museum, though in too fragile a condition to be regularly displayed.

Like his father, John Dillwyn Llewelyn was a keen botanist, building up the Penllergare estate into a picturesque romantic landscape with a rich variety of trees, shrubs and exotic plants, and with one of the first Orchid Houses in Britain. Towards the end of his life he gave 42 acres of Cnap Llwyd farm to Swansea, with £1,000 for it to be laid out as a park. This was named Parc Llewelyn, the first 'open space' for the people of Swansea. Though Penllergare mansion was demolished in 1961, and replaced by the offices of what was Lliw Valley Borough Council, the Penllergare Trust is active in restoring much of the estate for visitors to enjoy.

Amelia Earhart, *Wikipedia*

Memorial plaque

AMELIA EARHART

20 hours and 40 minutes

Those who stroll or jog along Llanelli's Millennium Coastal Path may pass a bi-lingual Blue Plaque in Pwll concerning the American aviator Amelia Earhart. On June 18th 1928 she had landed nearby, having become the first woman to fly across the Atlantic, a year after Lindbergh's solo flight. Although she was an experienced pilot who had secured the women's world altitude record of 14,000 ft in 1922, Earhart was not piloting the aircraft, but merely keeping the flight log, and she commented, 'I was just baggage, like a sack of potatoes. Maybe someday I'll try it alone'. With a pilot and a mechanic, she had flown from Newfoundland in an orange Fokker F7 named *Friendship* in 20 hours and 40 minutes. The pilot told a *Llanelli Mercury* reporter, 'We encountered fog almost all the way, and there was considerable rain as well. Most of the way I was flying blind because of the fog and rain. We had no idea where we were, as we had not seen Ireland. We landed here in South Wales because we were short of fuel.'

Among those who came out to congratulate her was the aviator Sir Arthur Whitten Brown, then living in Swansea, who had made the first non-stop transatlantic flight in 1919, along with Sir John Alcock. Amelia Earhart and the flight crew returned to the United States to a ticker-tape parade in New York, and reception with President Calvin Coolidge at the White House. Her first book *20 Hrs, 40 Min*, published later that year, was a journal of her experiences as the first woman passenger on a transatlantic flight.

In 1932 she did become the first woman to fly the Atlantic solo, and later that year the first woman to receive the Distinguished Flying Cross. Her achievement is also commemorated by engraved flagstones and a bi-lingual plaque in Burry Port harbour.

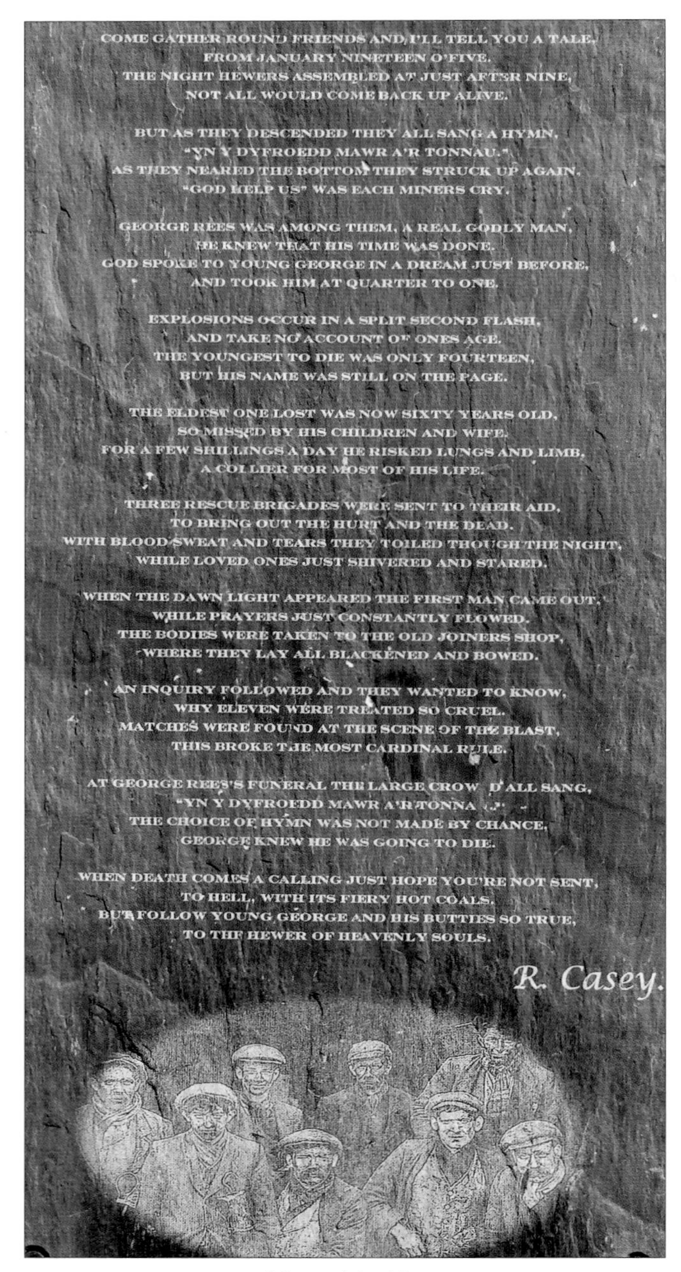

Memorial tablet

THE ELBA COLLIERY DISASTER

Mining tragedy: eleven lives lost

Collier and daughter
(Evan Evans)

October 14th 2013 was the centenary of the worst mining disaster in Britain, when 439 men and boys died in an explosion at the Universal Colliery, Senghenydd, near Caerphilly. Thankfully the Swansea area has had nothing on that scale, though during the 1904-05 religious revival which emanated from Moriah chapel, Loughor, a tragic mining accident occurred in Gowerton.

The Elba Colliery was a drift mine to provide fuel for the large Elba steelworks, connected by a private railway. Over 700 yards long, it was developed in 1881 to work the Swansea 3ft and 6ft seams: by 1900 150 men were working there. Two years later Baldwin's bought the mine and the steelworks, and by 1905 just the 6ft seam was being worked, to produce a hundred tons of coal each day. The mine was ventilated by a Waddle fan, manufactured in Llanelli.

On Friday, 20th January, 48 men, mostly from Penclawdd and Three Crosses, went underground at 5 p.m. at the start of the night shift. Just after midnight there was an explosion of coal gas, which produced a heavy fall. About thirty men rushed to help, though there was only room for six to work at a time clearing away rubble. Rescue attempts continued throughout the weekend, with the last body removed on the Monday.

Most of the men underground had suffered some degree of burns, and three casualties who were brought out alive died afterwards. In all eleven men and boys died, their ages ranging from 14 to 59. Three months earlier some of the doctors involved had also assisted nearby at the Loughor railway accident, when five men had died.

The subsequent enquiry heard that although a pipe and matches were found among the debris, the explosion was caused by a defective lamp rather than any attempt to smoke underground.

A memorial to the disaster is on the wall at the rear of St John's church car park in Gowerton. The Elba mine was abandoned, and the works later demolished, the area becoming the site for the 1980 National Eisteddfod.

Edgar Evans as a young cadet

Memorial postcard to the five who died

EDGAR EVANS

From the Sandfields to the South Pole

No blue plaque adorns Hoskins Place in Swansea – nor is a street name displayed there any longer. Hoskins Place runs off Little Gam Street, which joins Lower Oxford Street with Western Street, though nowadays it contains no dwellings. Its fame is that a young lad named Edgar Evans grew up there in the 1880s, before he joined the Royal Navy and went on to accompany Captain Scott on two expeditions to Antarctica. During the second of these, Petty Officer Evans stood with Scott at the South Pole, only to die on the return journey aged 35 – through hunger, exhaustion and inadequate nutrition in that most inhospitable of landscapes. In February 2012 the centenary of his death was commemorated with a civic service at St Mary's church in Swansea.

Edgar Evans was born in Rhossili but when he was seven the family moved into Swansea since his father, formerly a Cape Horner, found work with Bacon's Boats, which operated around the British Isles, and principally to Glasgow. While growing up in the Sandfields area, Edgar attended St Helen's School in Vincent Street, which has a framed photo of him in the hall. From the age of eleven Edgar was able to work part-time, on a type of work experience, as a telegraph messenger boy during the mornings, before returning to school for the afternoons.

Since his former home was demolished long ago, perhaps it is hardly appropriate to install a blue plaque in Hoskins Place stating that 'Petty Officer Edgar Evans, the first Welshman to reach the South Pole, lived near here before joining the Navy'. But his Swansea connections are remembered at St Helen's school and in Swansea Museum, which has a marble bust of him modelled on the 1912 photograph taken at the South Pole, while an exhibition and events marking the centenary of his death brought Swansea's Antarctic explorer to prominence.

Bethesda, Burry Green
(photo: Harold Grenfell)

Horton Chapel

GOWER CHAPELS' ANNIVERSARY

Two chapels – two centuries

2013 is the 200th anniversary of two Gower chapels – one in the north part of the peninsula and one in the south.

In the village of Burry Green stands Bethesda, the first of six non-conformist chapels built by Lady Barham, the former Diana Middleton, who settled at Fairy Hill in 1813. Bethesda churchyard contains the grave of Rev. William Griffiths, known as 'The Apostle of Gower', who built up the congregation in those early days. He preached throughout the peninsula, and lived at the Manse attached to the chapel, with responsibility at various times for the chapels in Penclawdd, Cheriton, Pilton Green (now a private house) and Oldwalls. William Griffiths was a Calvinistic Methodist, the denomination which is now called the Presbyterian Church of Wales. Burry Green's 150th anniversary service in 1963 was held in a marquee to accommodate the large number who came to hear the famous Welsh preacher, Dr Martyn Lloyd-Jones.

John Wesley was the founder of Methodism, which seceded from the Church of England after Wesley's death. Between 1764 and 1771 he made five visits to Oxwich, where he used to stay at the thatched cottage called 'The Nook'. South Gower has Wesleyan Methodist chapels at Mumbles, Murton, Horton, Pitton and Reynoldston, and there used to be others at Oxwich Green and Port Eynon. But it is Horton chapel that celebrates its bicentenary. Meetings were originally held at William Tucker's thatched farmhouse 'The Beeches', as Horton became the centre of Wesleyan Methodism in Gower. William Tucker donated the land on which the chapel was built, and it was opened free of debt two hundred years ago. It was later extended, and a Manse was built in the village around 1868.

Burry Green still has two services each Sunday, while at Horton the Sunday service alternates with Pitton chapel. Amid all the changes over two hundred years, these rural chapels of different Christian denominations still resonate to the worship of God.

Three Cliffs Nursing Home, Penmaen. The central block was the Gower Union Workhouse

THE GOWER UNION

Workhouse with a view

Three Cliffs Nursing Home in Penmaen commands a fine view over the south Gower cliffs and seems an idyllic location for the residents. But in Victorian times the prospect of living there would have evoked a reaction of horror – for it was the Gower Union Workhouse.

Charles Dickens' depiction of the Victorian workhouse in 'Oliver Twist' conveys much of the reality of those places. With their harsh regimes and separation of families they ensured that only the most destitute cases sought admission. Even John Merrick, the grossly disfigured 'Elephant Man', discharged himself from the Leicester workhouse, preferring to endure the revulsion of society at his appearance.

The central building of the Penmaen Union workhouse was built in 1861 at a cost of £3,866, to serve the needs of the 18 parishes that comprised the Gower Poor Law Union, established four years earlier. A new road was laid to provide access from what was then the turnpike road (now the south Gower road) towards Cefn Bryn.

Fifty inmates could be accommodated, with separate wards and exercise yards for men and women, for the sick and the infectious, and for vagrants. The sounding of a gong or bell would call residents to get up, to assemble for meals, and to go to bed.

The Master would inspect cleanliness and tidiness of dress for the men, and the Matron (often his wife) likewise for the women. At the 1881 census Penmaen had 29 residents, ten being over the age of 65, and eight being under the age of ten.

After the years of the Depression and the increase of unemployment, in 1929 legislation permitted local authorities to take over workhouse infirmaries as municipal hospitals. At Penmaen additional wings were added in 1939, and it became a place of care for the sick and the elderly, without the repressive regime of former times.

THEODORA. 77.77. From HANDEL'S *Theodora*, 1749.

A-men.

1 TAKE my life, and let it be
Consecrated, Lord, to Thee.
Take my moments and my days;
Let them flow in ceaseless praise.

2 Take my hands, and let them move
At the impulse of Thy love.
Take my feet, and let them be
Swift and beautiful for Thee.

3 Take my voice, and let me sing
Always, only for my King.
Take my lips, and let them be
Filled with messages from Thee.

4 Take my silver and my gold;
Not a mite would I withhold.
Take my intellect, and use
Every power as Thou shalt choose.

5 Take my will, and make it Thine;
It shall be no longer mine.
Take my heart—it is Thine own;
It shall be Thy royal throne.

6 Take my love; my Lord, I pour
At Thy feet its treasure-store.
Take myself, and I will be
Ever, only, all for Thee! Amen.

Frances Ridley Havergal, 1836-79.

Memorial plaque, Newton

FRANCES RIDLEY HAVERGAL

Her hymns live on

In the village of Newton, at the top of the hill that leads down to Caswell, a plaque in the wall of the house on the right states that the Christian poet and hymn-writer Frances Ridley Havergal lived and died there. Frances was in her early forties when she joined her elder sister Maria there in 1878, after the family home in Worcester had been sold following their step-mother's death. The family had visited Langland while on holiday, and rented from the Tuckers a new house then called *Park Villa*.

A fine musician and the daughter of an Anglican clergyman, Frances wrote 70 hymns (including one in French), and devotional books for children and adults. In her study where the west window looked over Caswell Bay stood her harp piano and her American typewriter, for she was constantly writing articles and checking proofs of verse and music. She enjoyed walking on the cliffs, going onto Caswell beach at low tide to explore the rock pools, watching the ships with all sails up entering Swansea harbour, and she was interested to visit Mumbles Lighthouse and speak with the lighthouse keeper. She became involved in temperance work, encouraging the young people to 'sign the pledge'. As St Peter's church in Newton was not built until after her death, Frances would attend Paraclete congregational chapel to play the organ and assist with the children's work.

She declined several proposals of marriage, and after a short illness died of peritonitis in June 1879, being buried in the family grave at Astley in Worcestershire, within sight of the Rectory where she had been born 42 years earlier.

Her hymns such as 'Who is on the Lord's side?' and 'Like a river glorious' are still sung today, especially 'Take my life and let it be' – which she preferred to be sung to a tune composed by her father, instead of the usual Mozart tune! Her Newton house *Park Villa* was renamed *Havergal*, and the plaque outside was unveiled in 1937 on the centenary of her birth, while nearby a street is named Havergal Close.

Sigmund Freud (left) with his biographer Ernest Jones

DR ERNEST JONES

Rescuer and biographer of Sigmund Freud

A blue plaque above the front door of a semi-detached house in Woodlands, Gowerton, states that it is the birthplace of the psychoanalyst Dr Ernest Jones. Born in 1879, he qualified as a doctor in 1900 after studying at Llandovery College and University College of Cardiff. Having read about Sigmund Freud's psychoanalytical approach in a German psychiatric journal, he began to use those techniques in dealing with mental illness, though the medical establishment was wary of this emphasis on the id and the libido, and he had to resign from his post at a London hospital.

In 1908 Jones organised the world's first psychiatric conference at Salzburg, when he first met Sigmund Freud, and he later wrote the major three-volume biography of him. While teaching in the department of psychiatry at the University of Toronto, Jones published psychoanalytical works on Hamlet and on dreams, and coined the term 'rationalisation'. He was twice president of the International Psychoanalytical Association, each time for several years, and was instrumental in the British Medical Association coming to officially recognise psychoanalysis in 1929. Before the outbreak of the Second World War, Jones bravely flew to Vienna to bring Freud and several other Jews to safety in London. His first wife was the talented Welsh musician, composer and mezzo-soprano, Morfydd Owen, who died tragically in Mumbles aged 26. He remarried the following year and had four children, including the writer Mervyn Jones.

Ernest Jones owned a holiday cottage Tŷ Gwyn, the former bakery in Llanmadoc, and after his death in 1958 his ashes were buried in Cheriton churchyard, in the grave of his seven-year-old daughter, and where his second wife was later buried. Fluent in German, the language of the early psychoanalysts, this Gowertonian became the first English-speaking psychoanalyst and its leading exponent in the English-speaking world.

Kennexstone Farmhouse at St Fagan's

KENNEXSTONE FARMHOUSE

A bit of Gower in St Fagan's

Until 62 years ago Kennexstone farmhouse in north-west Gower stood where the road from Llangennith joins the road to Llanmadoc.

In 1946 the Earl of Plymouth donated St Fagan's Castle near Cardiff, along with its garden and grounds, to the National Museum of Wales. Director Dr Iorwerth Peate envisioned an open-air Welsh folk museum there, like those he had seen in Scandinavia, with a building from each of the old counties of Wales. The building to come from Glamorgan would be Kennexstone farmhouse. In 1950 Dr Peate visited the Rogers family in Gower, and arranged to transfer their large stone-built farmhouse to St Fagan's.

The farmhouse had been built in three stages: in 1610 a single room on the ground floor with a bedroom above, to which was later added a large kitchen with a staircase leading to the upstairs sleeping area, with in the 1750s the addition of a back kitchen with a store-room above. Downstairs the box-bed by the fire was a particular feature of Gower homes.

The Welsh committee of the 1951 Festival of Britain awarded a grant to assist with the cost. A team of surveyors and builders stayed at the King's Head in Llangennith, numbering every stone and piece of timber as the building was dismantled. It took 38 lorry loads to move the farmhouse from Gower to St Fagan's in 1951. Much skilled work was needed – to rebuild the thatched roof required the expertise of a thatcher from Cardigan. The farmhouse was rebuilt, and furnished in a style from 1790, with the exterior painted red – customary at that time to protect the building and the occupants from evil spirits. A red-berried rowan tree was planted in the garden for the same reason.

When complete, Kennexstone farmhouse became in 1955 the fourth building to be opened to the public at what was then the Welsh Folk Museum (now known as the Museum of Welsh Life).

The barns that originally adjoined the farmhouse are now being moved to St Fagan's, to take their places among forty buildings at the Museum of Welsh Life.

Kilvrough Manor, Parkmill

The Gower Inn, Parkmill

Parkmill School

KILVROUGH MANOR

Pennard's grand estate

Behind the high, curving boundary wall alongside the road which leads downhill from Fairwood Common to Parkmill is the estate of Kilvrough.

The original mansion was built in 1585 by Rowland Dawkins whose grandson was one of the deputy Major Generals who ruled the country after the Civil War, when Cromwell was Lord Protector. After the restoration of the Monarchy, when Puritan minister John Myles was ejected from Ilston church, Dawkins allowed members of Wales's first Baptist church to meet on his land at Trinity Well in the Ilston Valley, before repressive legislation caused them to emigrate to the New World, founding Swanzey, Massachusetts.

The names of later members of the Dawkins family are inscribed on the eighteenth-century bells hung in Pennard church, though Rowland, who became Sheriff of Glamorgan, is spelt 'Daukin' on a bell dated 1737.

Kilvrough was remodelled later to a design of William Jernegan, before being purchased in 1820 by Major Thomas Penrice, who served as High Sheriff of Glamorgan in 1836. He built the Gower Inn in Parkmill and carried out restoration work at Pennard church in 1847. The estate passed to his nephew, another Thomas Penrice (High Sherriff in 1867), who acquired more land in Gower, built Parkmill School next to the Gower Inn, and introduced new farming methods to make Kilvrough one of the most productive estates in South Wales. He leased out the land at Pennard Burrows for a golf course before his death in 1896.

Kilvrough was left to his elder daughter Louisa, who married Admiral Algernon Lyons, becoming Lady Lyons when he was knighted. But with his death, the loss of their considerable German investments during the First World War, and heavy death duties after their eldest son's death of pneumonia in 1918, the estate had to be dispersed, and Kilvrough was sold two years later.

Lady Lyons later left Gower, but on her death aged 88 in 1935, like others of the Penrice and Lyons families, she was buried in the churchyard of St Mary's, Pennard.

Kilvrough was purchased by Oxfordshire County Council, and for several decades since then it has been used effectively as one of their residential centres for outdoor education.

Langland Bay Hotel, early 1900s

A poorly tinted version of the postcard

LANGLAND BAY HOTEL

Gower's 'Cyfarthfa Castle'

Why does an apartment block in Langland bear the name of a family of Merthyr Tydfil ironmasters? The site of the non-residential Langland Bay Hotel, which was demolished in the 1980s, is occupied by Crawshay Court.

Originally from Yorkshire, Richard Crawshay built up Cyfarthfa Ironworks in Merthyr Tydfil in the 1790s to become the largest in the world, and his grandson William erected Cyfarthfa Castle in 1824-25. William Crawshay's third son Henry earned the family's disapproval by marrying 'beneath his station', when he wed a foundry worker from Penderyn. Henry was placed in charge of the Cinderford ironworks in the Forest of Dean, which he managed successfully, and his family (they had at least 13 children) settled near Newnham in Gloucestershire.

In 1856 Henry had a summer villa built backing onto the Newton Cliffs, in a Scottish Baronial style. Originally known as Llan-y-Llan, this had a kitchen garden where the present car park in Langland stands. Henry died in 1879, and after his wife's death eight years later the estate was sold.

The building was expanded and enlarged into a luxury hotel for 150 guests, with tennis courts and a bowling green, and called the Langland Bay Hotel. But this was not a financial success, and the property was put up for sale in 1900, and again three years later. It was purchased in 1922 by the Workingmen's Club and Institute Union, for use as a convalescent home for miners and steelworkers – rather appropriate since their labour had provided the resources for it to be built.

A non-residential Langland Bay Hotel was built on the site of the coachman's house and outbuildings, and for many years this was popular for dances and wedding receptions. It was demolished in the 1980s, since when several hotels in the area like the Caswell Bay, the Osborne, the Langland Court and the St Anne's Hotel in Mumbles have all closed.

The miners' convalescent home was sold in 2005, and the Grade II listed building has been converted into 27 luxury apartments, known as Langland Bay Manor.

Saunders Lewis

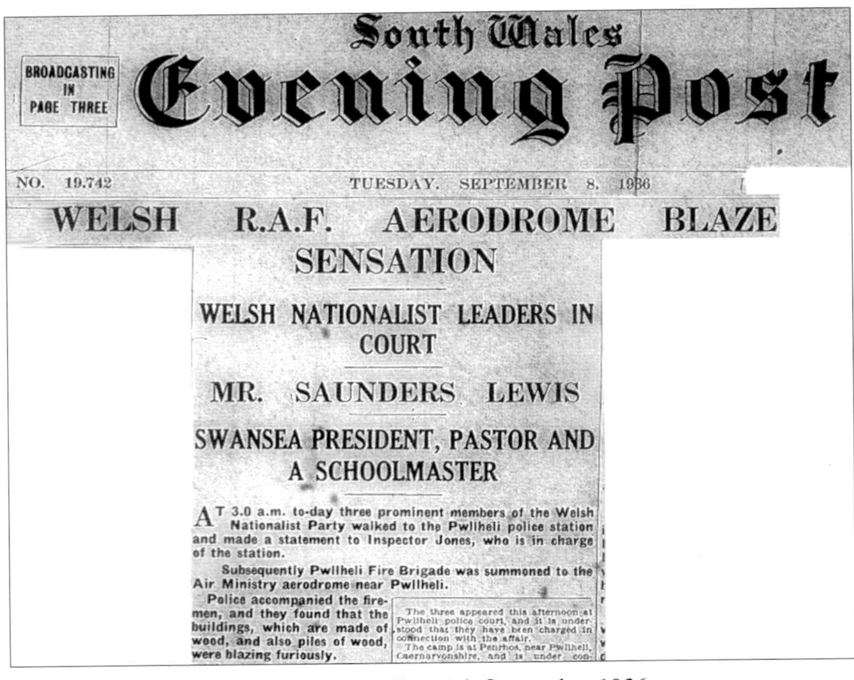

South Wales Evening Post

BROADCASTING IN PAGE THREE

NO. 19.742 TUESDAY, SEPTEMBER 8, 1936

WELSH R.A.F. AERODROME BLAZE SENSATION

WELSH NATIONALIST LEADERS IN COURT

MR. SAUNDERS LEWIS

SWANSEA PRESIDENT, PASTOR AND A SCHOOLMASTER

AT 3.0 a.m. to-day three prominent members of the Welsh Nationalist Party walked to the Pwllheli police station and made a statement to Inspector Jones, who is in charge of the station.

Subsequently Pwllheli Fire Brigade was summoned to the Air Ministry aerodrome near Pwllheli.

Police accompanied the firemen, and they found that the buildings, which are made of wood, and also piles of wood, were blazing furiously.

The three appeared this afternoon at Pwllheli police court, and it is understood that they have been charged in connection with the affair.

The camp is at Penrhos, near Pwllheli, Caernarvonshire, and is under con-

Evening Post headline, 8th September 1936

SAUNDERS LEWIS

Swansea's Welsh language martyr

Swansea University has had several notable members of staff since it became the fourth college of the University of Wales in 1920. Two years later Saunders Lewis, a founder and future president of Plaid Cymru, was appointed a lecturer in the Welsh department. But this major figure in Welsh literature was later to lose that position at the University in controversial circumstances.

In the 1930s the British government sought to establish an RAF bombing school first in Northumberland and then in Dorset, but had encountered vociferous protests in each area. Then Penyberth on the Llŷn peninsula in North Wales was chosen as the site. Despite a deputation representing half-a-million Welsh protesters, the Prime Minister refused to hear the case against siting the bombing school in North Wales. When the historic Penyberth farmhouse was destroyed ready for construction work, Saunders Lewis wrote that the British government seemed intent on turning a 'home of Welsh culture and literature into a place for promoting a barbaric method of warfare'.

In September 1936 Saunders Lewis, along with two other prominent Plaid Cymru members – teacher D. J. Williams and Welsh Baptist minister Lewis Valentine – set fire to sheds and building materials on the Penyberth site, before surrendering to the police. At Caernarfon Assizes a Welsh-speaking jury failed to agree on a verdict, but the trial was moved to the Old Bailey, where all three were sentenced to nine months' imprisonment at Wormwood Scrubs. Even before the verdict Saunders Lewis had been dismissed from his lectureship at Swansea University, an action which attracted widespread criticism. After serving their sentences, the three men returned to Caernarfon to great acclaim.

Subsequently Saunders Lewis wrote plays, poems and political commentaries, before becoming a Senior Lecturer in the Welsh department of University College, Cardiff. In 1962 he delivered the BBC Wales Annual Lecture, a major influence on the formation of Cymdeithas Yr Iaith Cymraeg (the Welsh Language Society).

This former Swansea University lecturer, who died in 1985, is regarded as one of the outstanding Welshmen of the twentieth century.

Dylan Thomas

THE LITTLE THEATRE

Little theatre, big history

Opposite the bowling green, the former Church Rooms of All Saints church in Mumbles opened in 1856 as a National (Anglican) School, and was augmented by a larger building in 1867 to the rear of The Prince of Wales pub. This building was later used by the Mumbles Motor Boat and Fishing Club. From 1929, the building was home to the newly-formed Swansea Stage Society, which four years later became the Swansea Little Theatre Players, with a young Dylan Thomas among their members.

After leaving the Grammar School, his theatrical abilities had been fostered working as a copy-reader at the *South Wales Daily Post* (since 1932 the *Evening Post*), which entailed reading reporters' copy aloud to the typesetters. Dylan's elder sister Nancy and her future husband Haydn Taylor were already members of the Little Theatre. In February 1932 all three had parts in Noël Coward's comedy 'Hay Fever'; the following year Dylan played the gaoler in 'The Merchant of Venice', with Wynford Vaughan Thomas as Lorenzo.

Before rehearsals in Mumbles, Dylan often had a drink at The Antelope or The Mermaid. If he had a minor role in a play, instead of waiting in the wings he would have a drink in The Prince of Wales, though always returning in time for his entrance. The Prince of Wales (now Patrick's) was then known as Cheese's, after Benny Cheese, landlord in the early 1900s.

Dylan left the Little Theatre in February 1934 after the producer had warned him that if he slipped out to the pub then he need not return – which is what happened. In spite of his abrupt departure, Dylan appeared with the company two months later for a one-night revival of 'Hay Fever' at the YMCA's Llewelyn Hall, and did similarly in 1936.

The Little Theatre moved from Mumbles to St Gabriel's Hall in Brynmill that year, then to other venues such as The Palace Theatre in 1956, before taking over the derelict former Oscar Chess car showroom near the Marina in 1970. After much renovation and rebuilding, it was opened by Sir Harry Secombe in 1983 as The Dylan Thomas Theatre, and for 30 years has been home to Swansea's community theatre.

During the

Strike

BUY YOUR

PROVISIONS

AT THE

Cheapest Stores

IN THE

United Kingdom.

CENTRIFUGAL

CREAMERY

BUTTER

Per **1/2** lb.

Perfect Quality.
The Produce of the
Richest Land in the
World.

MILD BREAKFAST

BACON

only **6½d.** per lb.

By the Side or Half
Side.

Best Value ever
offered.

Groceries of every
description at
Record Low Prices

ONLY ONE

BORO'

STORES

IT IS IN

College Street

Swansea.

DAVIES & Co.,

Proprietors.

Memorial plaque

TRAGIC EVENTS AT LLANELLY.

Soldiers Fire upon Crowd.

10 Men Shot Dead and Others Wounded.

A MOB'S VENGEANCE.

Goods Stolen and Trucks Fired.

Soldiers' Equipment Destroyed.

Gunpowder and Acetylene Explosions.

Ten Persons Dead and Dying, Scores Injured.

Magistrates' Shops Wrecked and Looted.

[illegible] of the towns affected by the railway strike has yielded victims [illegible] and furnished an amazing carnival of riot and pillage. It is a distinction [illegible] appreciated by self-respecting residents, who realise how the misdeeds of [illegible] small proportion of the inhabitants—and of outsiders, who are attracted [illegible] the vultures are to a carcase—may permanently reflect upon a whole [illegible]

The South Wales Daily Post, 20th August 1911

THE LLANELLI RAILWAY STRIKE

Soldiers fire on workers

In August 2011 a blue plaque was unveiled on the bridge near Copper-works School in Llanelli to commemorate the centenary of a railway strike that ended in tragedy. At that time railway workers were receiving very poor wages for a sixty to seventy-two hour working week, often with compulsory overtime.

When the first national railway strike took place, railway workers in Llanelli were joined in their protest by the better-paid tinplate workers and miners. As pickets were blocking the railway lines, troops were sent in to restore order, and for two days pitched battles raged between pickets and troops for the control of the line through the town. Then on 19th August the soldiers of the Worcester Regiment were ordered to fire on the strikers – and two were killed. One was a 21-year-old mill worker and promising rugby player, for scores of relatively well-paid tinplate workers had come out on the streets in solidarity with the rail workers. The other man killed was a 19-year-old labourer from London who was being treated at a sanatorium for tuberculosis, an endemic disease of the urban poor. He was spending his weekend leave in Llanelli. As news of the deaths spread, soldiers tried to restore order with fixed bayonets. Trucks of the railway company were attacked and set on fire, a man was killed when a railway truck exploded, and the following day three more people died from their injuries.

Lloyd George, the Chancellor of the Exchequer, persuaded railway bosses to agree to a commission of inquiry into the industry, and that was enough to satisfy the union leaders, who called off the strike. The railway workers had won better pay and conditions, though the main result was to provide an impetus towards organisational unity, with the National Union of Railwaymen being established two years later, the forerunner of today's RMT (Rail, Maritime and Transport Workers) Union.

The Church of St Cyfelach and St David, Llangyfelach

LLANGYFELACH CHURCH

The rebel vicar

In West Wales the ten bells of St David's Cathedral are housed in a thirteenth century bell tower adjoining the Tower Gate House, which overlooks the Cathedral with its large central tower.

Likewise at Llangyfelach the tower that houses their four bells is detached from and overlooks the church. This came about through damage to the mediaeval church building after a gale in 1805. Instead of the church being repaired, the nearby tithe barn was converted into the nave of a new Llangyfelach church, and the old building was demolished around 1830. So, as at St David's Cathedral, the Llangyfelach bell tower stands alone, without any tower attached to the church.

A small brass plaque from the old church is in the new one. This is in memory of the parents of Marmaduke Matthews, born at Nydfwch Farm in 1606. He studied for the ministry at All Souls, Oxford, and during the turbulent years leading up to the Civil War he became Vicar of Penmaen, where his Puritan leanings and radical preaching were too challenging for some parishioners.

Seeking religious liberty like the Pilgrim Fathers, Matthews and his wife emigrated to Massachusetts in the New World in 1636. But he remained in correspondence with the parliamentarian Colonel Philip Jones (also from Llangyfelach), who encouraged him to return to Wales under Oliver Cromwell's Protectorate.

After 16 years in North America, Matthews returned to become vicar of St John's church in Swansea's High Street (subsequently rebuilt and re-dedicated to St Matthew). However, with the restoration of the Monarchy, Matthews was ejected in 1662 from his church, along with many others such as John Myles in Ilston, and notably John Bunyan in Bedford.

Even without the security of a regular stipend for a minister of the Established Church, Marmaduke Matthews continued to minister to groups of dissenters until his death around 1683. His former home Tirdwncyn became an early centre of nonconformist worship in the area, from which Mynyddbach chapel and many others grew.

Horse power

Near the end of the line

Train and pier

THE MUMBLES RAILWAY

Loved but lost

One of three rusty poles near the Square Café in Oystermouth Square might seem of no interest, yet it is a tangible, albeit humble, reminder of the world's first passenger railway. Following an 1804 Act of Parliament, the Oystermouth Railway began to transport limestone quarried locally and coal from the Clyne valley by horse-drawn wagons to Swansea. Then from March 1807 passengers were carried to a regular timetable along the 4½-mile route, making this the world's first passenger railway. That venture was suspended around 1827 when a turnpike road between Swansea and Oystermouth was constructed, but passengers were again carried on the railway from 1860, until the much-lamented closure of the line on 5th January 1960.

From originally being horse-drawn, the Oystermouth Railway changed to steam locomotion from 1877 (although for nearly 20 years steam power was used alongside horse power!), before the line was electrified in 1929. Double-deck passenger cars built in Loughborough and carrying 106 passengers were introduced, with overhead transmission – hence the pole in Oystermouth Square. The line ended at Oystermouth until an embankment was constructed to carry the line on to Mumbles Head; this extension was opened in 1898, at the same time as Mumbles pier. The embankment enclosed what had been the natural harbour known as Horsepool, which was filled in and later built upon. From the depot at Rutland Street, the trains had nine stops, with the last being at Mumbles Pier.

Since the line's closure, Mumbles Road has been greatly widened for traffic, with the creation of the footpath and cycle path along the foreshore. In the Tramshed in the Maritime Quarter the front end of red passenger car number 7 is displayed, while other reminders of the Railway include the former Blackpill station and electricity sub-station with its colonnaded porch (now The Junction Café), and less obviously that rusty pole in Oystermouth Square.

St Illtyd Church, Ilston

Trinity Well, Ilston Valley – the first Baptist Church in Wales

JOHN MYLES

Gower's Pilgrim Father

From the Gower Inn at Parkmill a wooded path leads up the valley to the hamlet of Ilston. Only a short distance from the pub car park, after crossing a bridge there is a stone pulpit on the right, with a tablet which David Lloyd George unveiled in 1928. This commemorates Rev. John Myles, who established the first Baptist church in Wales, although it says nothing about any American connection.

After the end of the English Civil War and the execution of King Charles I, a Herefordshire man named John Myles, of Puritan leanings, became minister of Ilston church. He organised the congregation on Baptist lines to become only the second nonconformist church in Wales, and the membership grew to 261. But eleven years later, after the death of Oliver Cromwell, the monarchy was restored when Charles II returned from exile. In a reaction against Puritan reforms many ministers were ejected from their pulpits, to be replaced by clergy who adhered to the rites and practices of the Established Church.

Among those ejected was John Bunyan, who while imprisoned in Bedford jail began to write the classic *Pilgrim's Progress*, and John Myles, whose followers moved from Ilston church to worship on private land in Trinity Well, near the ruins of a pre-reformation chapel. When repressive legislation made life increasingly difficult for dissenters, Myles sought religious freedom in the New World, as the Pilgrim Fathers had done forty years earlier. With 18 of his congregation Myles sailed from Bristol to North America, and landed at Boston before establishing the first 'Swansea' overseas in the present-day state of Massachusetts. This settlement was on the edge of the frontier, and survived an Indian attack in 1674, when colonial troops were garrisoned at Myles' house, and the church and part of the town were destroyed. John Myles died aged 63 and was buried in Providence, Rhode Island.

Nowadays although the plaque omits any mention of Swansea, Massachusetts, the Ilston memorial is frequently visited by American Baptists, grateful for 'Gower's Pilgrim Father'.

The old church

(George Halliday)

The restored church

(Walter Goddard)

St Nicholas, Nicholaston today

NICHOLASTON CHURCH

The 'Cathedral of Gower'

Nicholaston church stands in isolation beside the main south Gower road. Originally dating from the 14th century, St Nicholas church was completely rebuilt in 1894 in Anglo-Catholic style, and was described by Rev. J. D. Davies, rector of Llanmadoc and Cheriton, as 'the most elaborately treated ecclesiastical building in Wales, if not in the west of England'.

The cost of the rebuilding was borne by Olive Talbot, third daughter and youngest child of C. R. M. Talbot of Penrice and Margam. He had built Margam Castle, and after over 50 years in Westminster became 'Father of the House of Commons'. On his death in 1890, Olive used her inheritance to build and restore a number of churches. In Maesteg and Abergwynfi new churches were built, while others in the Maesteg area and at Nicholaston were restored or enlarged.

To rebuild St Nicholas church in memory of C. R. M. Talbot cost more than £2,000 (over three-and-a-half million pounds today). Stone from Cefn Bryn was used for rebuilding the walls. Materials used for the interior included teak and oak, alabaster and coloured marble. The font is said to be made from a solid block of stalagmite, and the hanging pulpit (as opposed to one attached to the floor) is decorated with alabaster figures of Keble, Pusey and Liddon. These three 'High Churchmen' were prominent in the Oxford Movement, which during the 19th century sought to re-introduce ritual and ceremonial into the services of the Church of England.

Olive Talbot never saw any of these buildings completed, for she died in London in 1894, just before her 52nd birthday, after living for the previous 20 years as an invalid at 3 Cavendish Square. Spinal injuries had even prevented her from attending her father's funeral in Margam Abbey, where in the family vault she was subsequently buried. Two months after her death, Nicholaston church re-opened in December 1894, with a tablet on the north wall expressing gratitude to Olive Talbot for the rebuilding.

Morfydd Owen

MORFYDD OWEN

Outstanding musician dies at twenty-six

Next to the house in Thistleboon, Mumbles, which belongs to Catherine Zeta-Jones and her husband Michael Douglas, is an older house called Craig-y-môr. There in 1918 the Gowerton-born psychoanalyst Dr Ernest Jones brought his wife Morfydd Llwyn Owen, who was from Treforest, for a holiday in Gower. They visited Caswell, Langland, Sketty, and Swansea Market, before Morfydd was taken ill with appendicitis, necessitating an operation. Instead of taking her to Swansea Infirmary, it seems the operation took place at Craig-y-môr. Tragically chloroform instead of ether was used as the anaesthetic, and Morfydd Owen died, just weeks before her 27th birthday.

An Associate of the Royal Academy of Music, Morfydd Owen was an outstanding mezzo-soprano and one of Wales' most gifted composers and musicians. She composed choral works, chamber music, piano and orchestral works, songs and hymn tunes. A Welsh speaker, she had been admitted to the Gorsedd of Bards at the National Eisteddfod at Wrexham in 1912. Friends from the Welsh Presbyterian chapel in Charing Cross were shocked by her marriage to Ernest Jones, an atheist with a flamboyant lifestyle, at a time when psychoanalysis was viewed with suspicion. Jones had proposed on their third meeting, and they were married at Marylebone registry office, with her parents absent – as the wedding took place a day earlier than planned! Seven months later, however, there was a ceremony at Charing Cross chapel at which her parents could be present.

Dr and Mrs Jones had been married for 18 months when Morfydd died. Her grave at the top of Oystermouth cemetery is marked with a red sandstone column bearing a quotation from Goethe's *Faust*, for German was the language of Freud and the leading psychoanalysts. In translation this can be rendered 'Here the indescribable consequences (of love) have been fulfilled'. Her obituary in *Y Gorlan* commented: 'Oh, Death! we knew that thou were blind, but in striking Morfydd thou hast taught us that thou art also deaf'.

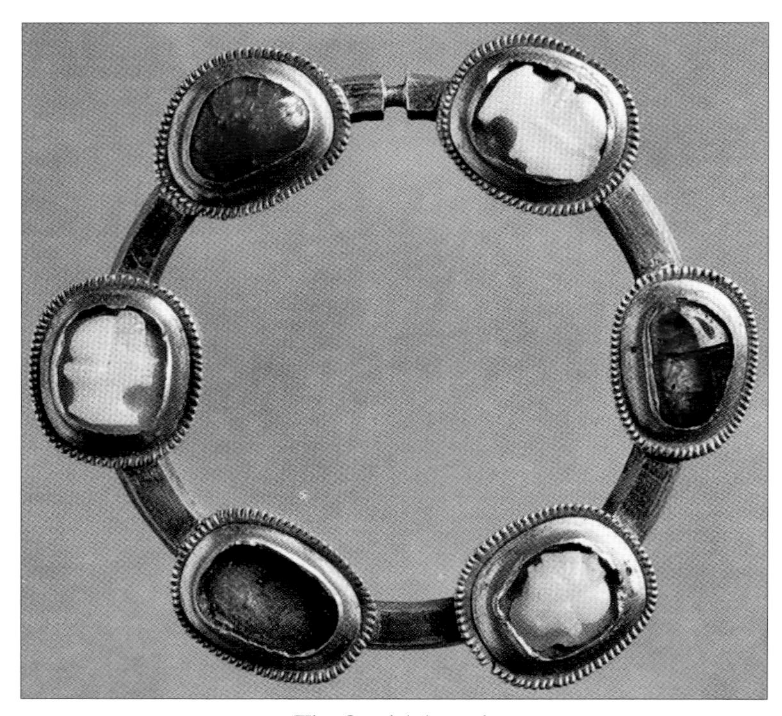

The Oxwich brooch

THE OXWICH BROOCH

Royal chicken-feed

How did a King of England's ring-brooch come to be in Oxwich castle?

The castle is hidden among the trees just off the road that leads uphill from Oxwich to Oxwich Green. Rather than a traditional stone castle it is a fortified manor house built during Tudor times. The two-storey building was erected on the site of an earlier castle, with an impressive six-storey block added some thirty years later.

When in 1949 the Ministry of Public Buildings and Works announced plans to reduce its walls to the height of the earlier building, the recently-formed Gower Society led the protest, and the decision was reversed. For many years while restoration work intermittently took place the castle remained closed to the public. The two-storey building had been used as a farmhouse, and in 1968 workmen were surprised to find that some hens had unearthed a gold ring-brooch dating from medieval times. This 40mm diameter brooch, with six elaborate settings, may have belonged to Edward II, the subject of Marlowe's drama of 1592.

His father Edward I was the warrior-king who conquered Scotland and North Wales, but Edward II was a weak character, unsuited to lead Britain in those days. As the country descended into anarchy, Edward fled to South Wales in 1326, vainly hoping for suitable weather to sail to refuge in Lundy Island. Having sent charters, jewellery, money, weapons and clothing ahead to Swansea castle, he was captured near Llantrisant and deposed, later to be murdered in Berkeley castle. Certain royal possessions were purloined from Swansea castle, and suspicion fell on Robert de Penres (of Penrice and Oxwich), though nothing could be proved.

In the mid-19th century Edward II's marriage contract from 1303 was found in Gower, and presented to Swansea Museum, where for many years it used to be on display. Did the gold ring-brooch that was uncovered in Oxwich castle, and which is now displayed in Cardiff's National Museum of Wales, also belong to this most unsuitable of English kings?

Above: Silver denarius of Carausius Adventus

Left: Bronze Carausius coin, reverse, with clasped hands and abbreviation RSR

(Redeunt Saturnia Regna – "The Golden Ages have Returned")

Southgate, with the Post Office on the right

THE PENNARD HOARD

Roman treasure trove in Gower

In the village of Southgate the road from the car park near the bus terminus, which goes along Pennard cliffs in the direction of Three Cliffs Bay, is called Westcliff. Behind those houses with the fine view across to North Devon, and running parallel to Westcliff, is Heatherslade Close.

A Roman hoard of the same period from Frome

As the houses in that Close were being built in the 1960s, a surprising discovery was made when a septic tank was being installed. A worn bronze bowl was uncovered and found to contain a large number of coins, welded together by corrosion. There were 2,583 Roman coins, dating from the period of Valerian, who became Roman Emperor in the year 253AD, up to the time of the Emperor Carausius, who died in 293. These coins date from over seven centuries before the battle of Hastings – roughly 1,700 years ago. Of course, compared to the time of the Red Lady of Paviland, they are fairly recent!

Does this mean that the Romans were in Pennard? Roman pottery has been found in Minchin Hole, near Southgate car park, and it seems that a Roman villa was near or on the site of Oystermouth church. But the mere location of coins is inconclusive, for they could have been carried some distance, and they might have been buried at a later date. We know that the cliffs and caves in Gower were occupied during Roman times by people in contact with centres of the Roman occupation, such as at Loughor.

The fact that the coins were in a bronze bowl suggests that they were deliberately concealed, presumably with the intention of being recovered later, though this did not happen. That place of burial might have been chosen because an end-on view of Cefn Bryn could have provided a sighting-point for locating where the coins were concealed.

To walk along Heatherslade Close today one would hardly believe that such a large hoard of Roman coins had been discovered nearby.

St Andrew's Church, Penrice. The 'murder stone' is near the left of the tower

A PENRICE GRAVESTONE

Murder by persons unknown

The village of Penrice in peninsular Gower seems an idyllic place, with cottages and church grouped around the green, and a splendid view across the fields to Oxwich Bay. Yet outside the porch of St Andrew's church stands a grave that suggests things used to be rather different.

It is the grave of Mary Kavanagh and it bears the inscription 'Here lies Mary, wife of John Kavanagh of Penmaen, who was murdered by ——— on 3 Oct. 1829, aged 75 years'. She was predeceased by both her husband and her son, who are buried nearby, and it seems strange that an elderly widow was murdered in the quiet hamlet of Penrice. However, in those days the annual Penrice Fair could be a riotous occasion, with prize-fighting and much drunkenness, with inebriated persons sometimes being laid out on graves to 'sleep it off'. Perhaps an attempted robbery had turned violent?

An actual 'murder stone' stands outside Cadoxton church near Neath, having the word MURDER at the top, and the warning: 'Although the SAVAGE MURDERER escape for a season the detection of man, yet GOD hath set his mark on him either for time or eternity, and the cry of blood will assuredly pursue him to certain and terrible but righteous JUDGEMENT'.

That was for the 1822 murder of 26-year-old Margaret Williams from Carmarthenshire, who was in service. A man was arrested on suspicion of her murder, but released through lack of evidence in those pre-DNA times, and he later moved to America. Her grave is beside the footpath through the churchyard, at an angle where it would be noticed by passers-by. For the words were intended to awaken the conscience of the murderer, as well as serving as a warning to others.

Nebo chapel in Felindre has similar words on a gravestone following the murder of a 29-year-old woman who lived in Llangyfelach. Of course all this happened long before a police force was established.

MV Shanklin, later renamed *Prince Ivanhoe*

Aground at Horton

PRINCE IVANHOE

Grounded at Horton

When Mumbles pier opened in 1898 it contained a landing stage for passengers to board ships for pleasure cruises, such as the paddle steamer *Brighton* or the *Glen Gower.* Many readers will recall The White Funnel Fleet of the Bristol-based company P & A Campbell. Until recently there were still pleasure cruises along the south Gower coast or to Ilfracombe or Lundy Island, in *Waverley*, the last sea-going paddle steamer in the world or in *Balmoral*, though departing from Swansea's King's Dock rather than from Mumbles pier. But in 1981 one pleasure cruise along the south Gower coast ended in disaster on Horton beach.

The M.V. *Shanklin* had been launched on Clydeside in 1951, and for thirty years provided a ferry service between Portsmouth and Ryde in the Isle of Wight. After being renovated by the Firth of Clyde Steam Packet Company for pleasure cruises, she was re-named *Prince Ivanhoe* after the hero of Sir Walter Scott's novel. On her first excursion along the south Gower coast on 3rd August 1981 she sailed close to Port Eynon Point during the afternoon, and struck a submerged object – possibly a submerged wreck. Since she was taking on water from a 25-metre gash in her hull, *Prince Ivanhoe* was run aground on Horton beach, so that the 450 passengers could be brought ashore, using an RAF air-sea rescue helicopter, with lifeboats from Horton, Port Eynon and Mumbles. Two persons suffered heart attacks, one of whom was declared dead on arrival at hospital.

Salvage attempts during subsequent years removed much of the wreck, though part still remains, and for many years two orange buoys marked the area of the shipwreck.

In her earlier role as M.V. *Shanklin*, the ship had collided with Ryde Pier on three occasions; on one of these in 1973 amid heavy fog she destroyed 40 feet of the pier's roadway, causing a taxi to sink into the water, although there were no casualties. Evidently a later change of name failed to improve her safety record.

Prince's Fountain

SWANSEA'S WELCOME TO KING AND QUEEN.

THEIR MAJESTIES RECEIVE A MAGNIFICENT WELSH GREETING

SCENES AT THE SOD-CUTTING CEREMONY.

KING BESTOWS A KNIGHTHOOD ON MR. GRIFFITH THOMAS.

TOWN ABLAZE WITH SUPERB DECORATIONS.

ROYAL TRIUMPHAL PROGRESS THROUGH ABERTAWE'S STREETS.

KING AND THE VETERANS: QUEEN AND THE SCHOOLBOY.

MARCH OF THE SEAMEN AND MARINES.

LONDON CRITICS ASTONISHED AT SWANSEA'S ENTHUSIASM.

He returned to Swansea as King in 1904
to open the King's Dock

THE PRINCE'S FOUNTAIN

Royal wedding celebrated in Mumbles

Near the William Hancock pub in Mumbles (formerly the Waterloo Hotel) stands a stone drinking fountain that commemorates the wedding of Queen Victoria's eldest son, the future Edward VII. The Prince's Fountain was erected in 1863, following the wedding at St George's Chapel, Windsor, of 21-year-old Edward, Prince of Wales, to 18-year-old Princess Alexandra of Denmark.

The celebration of this Royal Wedding was somewhat muted, as the Queen was still in mourning for Prince Albert, who had died fourteen months earlier. At the service ladies were restricted to wearing grey, lilac or mauve. The Queen watched from a special box high in the chapel, and did not attend the wedding breakfast.

Like the present Prince of Wales, Prince Edward had a long wait after his marriage until he ascended to the throne, but during this time of waiting he was not permitted to exercise any royal power. His lavish lifestyle did not meet with Queen Victoria's approval, for he ran up huge gambling debts, had liaisons with various ladies such as the actress Lillie Langtry, and was nearly named as co-respondent in a Member of Parliament's divorce suit. Thirty-eight years after his wedding Prince Edward became King Edward VII, and, notwithstanding his lack of experience in carrying out royal duties, he was an effective King during a reign of nearly a decade.

As Prince of Wales he had visited Swansea in 1881 to open Swansea's third dock – the Prince of Wales Dock – which is now the focus of the SA1 development. Edward returned as King in 1904 with Queen Alexandra to perform the ceremony of 'cutting the first sod' of the new King's Dock (which was opened in 1909). Swansea's King Edward Road in Brynmill was named in his honour, just as Alexandra Road (and in London the original Alexandra Palace, opened four months after their marriage) had been named after his consort.

St Helen's ground
(Swanseatilidie, Wikipedia)

Statue of Sir Garfield (Garry) Sobers at the Kensington Oval, Barbados
(Winton Edghill, Wikipedia)

ST HELEN'S GROUND

Great sporting memories

St Helen's rugby and cricket ground opened in 1873, and first staged first-class cricket in 1921, when Glamorgan became the 17th county to enter the county championship. With its sandy subsoil, St Helen's is considered one of the fastest drying grounds in the country.

It has been the venue of several historic matches, notably Glamorgan's victory over the Australians in 1964. R. B. Simpson's team came to Swansea that August undefeated, having retained the 'Ashes' by drawing the fourth Test, but were beaten by a team containing no current test players. This gave Glamorgan a 'full set' of victories over each of the test-playing countries at that time. To prove this was no fluke, on the next Australian tour four years later they were again beaten at St Helen's by Glamorgan, captained by Port Eynon-born Don Shepherd. A few weeks later it was at St Helen's that the great West Indian cricketer Garfield Sobers, playing for Nottinghamshire, became the first player to hit the maximum six sixes in an over of a first-class match. (A feat that can still be watched on *You Tube*.)

But once Glamorgan had purchased their own ground in Cardiff at Sophia Gardens, it was that ground that became the focus of development, and first-class cricket in Swansea was scaled down to merely a few matches a year, in spite of the efforts of the Balconiers. The Cardiff ground was developed into the Swalec Stadium, and since 2009 it has staged test matches. At the Mumbles end of St Helen's, rugby internationals took place from 1882 to 1954, and there the New Zealand All Blacks suffered their first defeat by a club side – Swansea winning 11-3 in 1935. More recently in 1992 at St Helen's, Swansea achieved victory against the World Cup holders Australia by 21-6.

Though Cardiff is now Wales's city for international rugby and test cricket, St Helen's, Swansea, has a proud record of outstanding matches in both sports.

Alfred Sisley

ALFRED SISLEY

Bay creates an impression

In an exhibition of French Impressionist paintings one might be surprised to recognise a Langland feature among paintings of Alfred Sisley. A few years ago his paintings were part of an exhibition at the National Gallery in London's Trafalgar Square, and at the National Museum of Wales. The feature is Storr's Rock on Rotherslade beach, which attracted Sisley's notice while he was staying at the Osborne Hotel in 1897 with his wife, for he included that rock in several paintings.

Sisley was an Englishman born in Paris, whose only visits outside France were to Britain. In his views of the rock on Rotherslade beach he calls it Storr's Rock, and in all those paintings he refers to Rotherslade Bay as Lady's Cove. Perhaps Storr's is simply Sisley's version of Rother's Tor, and Ladies' Cove may have been the name given to Rotherslade Bay by the Osborne Hotel staff. In those days of segregated bathing, Rotherslade Bay was usually reserved for ladies, while men would have been directed to swim in Langland. In the summer of 1897, Sisley embarked on what was a final visit to Britain. Following a brief stay in London and Cornwall, he took lodgings at Penarth with his long-term partner (they had two children), whom he married at Cardiff's registry office. They moved on to Langland Bay, and stayed at the Osborne Hotel.

Sisley and the Impressionists would paint landscapes in the open air, rather than in a studio. At Rotherslade, enthralled by windy cliffs, Sisley captured the distinctive light effects on the sea and the tidal ranges, as in *Lady's Cove, Langland Bay, Morning*, and the waves crashing against Storr's Rock, as in *Storr's Rock, Lady's Cove, Evening* or *Storr's Rock, Rotherslade Bay from below the Osborne Hotel.* These Welsh landscapes were to be among his last paintings, for he died a year later in his sixtieth year.

The Osborne Hotel was demolished in 2003 and replaced by the Osborne Apartments.

Study for Dylan Thomas, watercolour by Chris Last

DYLAN THOMAS

The man and the myth

When on St David's Day 1982 Dylan Thomas's memorial was unveiled in Poets' Corner in Westminster Abbey, there was little in Swansea to show that the city was the birthplace of this major twentieth century poet. By contrast, in Laugharne those who enjoyed *Under Milk Wood*, his 'play for voices', could visit the Old Boathouse where Dylan had lived, Brown's Hotel which he frequented, and St Martin's church where he was buried.

Much of the impetus to recognise Dylan Thomas in Swansea stemmed from Londoner Jeff Towns, who assembled the superb collection of memorabilia 'Dylan Thomas: Man and Myth' for display in what used to be the Old Guildhall. That building had been erected 1825-29, before enlargement 25 years later, but had become nearly derelict prior to modern rebuilding as Tŷ Llên (House of Literature) for 1995, when Swansea hosted the UK Year of Literature and Writing. Subsequently renamed The Dylan Thomas Centre, it now attracts people from around the world to the annual Dylan Thomas Festival. Swansea has numerous other reminders of Dylan, such as the Ronald Cour stone and the Memorial Shelter in Cwmdonkin Park, the bronze statue with lines from 'Fern Hill' in the Marina, near the statue of Captain Cat (from *Under Milk Wood*), the stained glass leaf in Castle Square with a quote around the base of the fountain, and Dylan's birthplace, 5 Cwmdonkin Drive, which is open for guided tours.

Little of the old Grammar School that he attended on Mount Pleasant Hill remains, and nothing of the old *Evening Post/Herald of Wales* building in front of Swansea Castle where Dylan worked in 1931/32, nor of 'Ralph the Books' near the railway station, nor of the Three Lamps that he patronised (among other places). Perhaps one day a plaque on Y Llannerch in The Grove in the Uplands could state that the 1949 BBC programme discussing 'Swansea and the Arts' and chaired by Dylan was recorded there. While one might not endorse his lifestyle, the memory of this writer, poet and broadcaster is prominent in his 'ugly, lovely town'.

RMS *Titanic* at Southampton Docks, April 1912

Titanic sinking, coloured engraving by Willy Stöwer

TITANIC TRAGEDY

City connections

Numerous books, films and documentaries remind us that on 14 April 1912 on her maiden voyage R.M.S. *Titanic* struck an iceberg in the north Atlantic, and sank nearly three hours later. One might assume that maritime disaster has no connection with this locality, but that is not the case.

There is a memorial in Cadoxton church near Neath to Robert Leyson, a 24-year-old mining engineer who was a second-class passenger. The son of a Swansea solicitor, he was travelling to New York to join his brother Thomas in business. His body was one of 306 recovered by the cable ship *Mackay-Bennett*, which had been chartered by the White Star Line to recover bodies. Leyson's was one of 116 bodies which were then buried at sea. He had been identified because his keys had his name on them, and he also had a silver case containing £4 – a considerable sum when the second-class ticket cost ten guineas.

Owen Wilmore Samuel was related to the 'Samuel' of the firm Astley Samuel Leeder. He had worked in the large Ben Evans department store, which before the Blitz stood on what is now Castle Square. Aged 41 and married with a child, Samuel lived in Southampton. He had previously served in the *Oceanic*, and was a steward in the *Titanic*'s second-class saloon. His body was also recovered by the *Mackay-Bennett*, but he was buried, along with many others from *Titanic*, in the cemetery in Halifax, Nova Scotia, on 8 May.

Survivors included a 26 year-old steward named William C. Foley from Fisher Street (the southern section of present-day Princess Way). Born in Swansea, he had embarked from Queenstown (now Cobh) in Ireland, and as a third-class steward earned three pounds fifteen shillings per month. A member of the crew of lifeboat No. 13, he was rescued by the *Carpathia*, and disembarked at New York on 18 April.

Less fortunate were miners William Rogers from Alltwen and Evan Davies from Bryncoch: both were travelling third-class hoping for work in America, but they were drowned, along with 1,500 others in the early hours of 15 April 1912.

Clyne Castle, Graham Vivian's home

GRAHAM VIVIAN

Swansea's reclusive financier

Clyne Castle was known as Woodlands when built in 1791, before being re-modeled by later owners, especially from 1860 by Graham Vivian, second son of the industrialist John Henry Vivian. While elder brother Henry Hussey Vivian took over the day-to-day running of the Hafod copper works, Graham was an astute financier who amassed a fortune with shrewd investments, especially in railway companies. When he died in 1912, he left a fortune worth £130 million in today's money.

Fluent in French, German and Italian, he made extensive alterations to the property which he renamed Clyne Castle, filling it with antiques, paintings, busts, tapestries, and porcelain from his continental travels. Though somewhat reclusive and, unlike his father and elder brother (both of whom were MPs) not involved in public service, Graham Vivian welcomed to Clyne Castle's 50 rooms such persons as Lord Palmerston, Winston Churchill, Adelina Patti and the future Edward VII and Queen Alexandra, when they opened the Prince of Wales Dock in 1881. He organised shoots for his guests at Clyne and the Parc le Breos estate.

A bachelor, Graham Vivian declined to have a telephone installed at Clyne Castle, and never purchased a motor-car, preferring to travel by a coach and horses. When in his eighties he had Clyne chapel built, it was not facing east, had no stained glass lest that distract from the beauty of its surroundings, and he stipulated there should be no high-church ritual in the services. One of his final public appearances was in 1911 to open the Glynn Vivian Art Gallery, on behalf of his deceased younger brother. He died the following year, leaving Clyne to his unmarried sister Dulcie during her lifetime, and then to their nephew Admiral Walker-Heneage-Vivian.

In the 1950s University College Swansea acquired Clyne Castle, adapting it as a hall of residence called Neuadd Gilbertson, while the City of Swansea acquired Clyne Gardens. With over 2,000 different plants including over 800 rhododendrons, Clyne Gardens was open to the public just one day a year during Graham Vivian's time, but now it can be enjoyed throughout the year on any day.

Cliff-top memorial

Memorial in St Mary's Pennard

VERNON WATKINS

Poet in a bank

At the junction of St Helen's Road and Beach Street stands the premises of Messrs. William Hill, but this building used to be the St Helen's Road branch of Lloyds Bank, where a few decades ago a customer might encounter 'the poet of Gower' – Vernon Watkins.

Having curtailed his Cambridge studies of modern languages, Vernon suffered a nervous breakdown after beginning work as a bank clerk in Grangetown, Cardiff. He was transferred to Swansea's St Helen's Road branch so he could live with his parents at what is now the Heatherslade Bay Rest Home in Pennard, travelling to work each day by bus. After marriage to Gwen, whom he met during the war at Bletchley Park, the government code-breaking centre, Vernon lived at 'The Garth' on Pennard cliffs. At work he was always a gentlemanly clerk – in the days when bank staff did not have to try to sell insurance or other services to customers only wanting to pay in a cheque.

His thoughts may often have been on metaphysical poetry, for there was an occasion when Vernon left the bank unlocked at the end of the working day! Fortunately a Doctor Who-style police box used to be sited opposite outside Swansea Infirmary (which is now Home Gower), and the premises were secured by a kindly policeman.

Vernon died in Seattle in 1967 at the age of 61, on his second term as Visiting Professor of Literature at the University of Washington, and there are memorials to him inside Pennard church and on the cliff top overlooking Hunts Bay. This was a favourite spot where he would look across to Oxwich Bay and find inspiration for his poetry.

Though Vernon is not as famous as his friend Dylan Thomas, his poetry is of a high quality, and some years ago it was the subject of a Swansea University lecture – given by former Archbishop of Canterbury, Dr Rowan Williams, who presented a Radio Three programme in 2012 on Vernon entitled 'Swansea's Other Poet'.

Whiteford Lighthouse

WHITEFORD LIGHTHOUSE

'One of only a handful in the world'

Having been in operation since 1793, Mumbles lighthouse is Gower's prominent lighthouse, though another stands on the north-west corner of the peninsula, but which no longer operates. This lighthouse is at Whiteford Point, and strangely is the second one to be built there.

The first Whiteford lighthouse was erected in 1854 on timber piles, but was liable to damage from drifting wreckage and collisions from boats. In 1865 it was replaced 317 yards further south, by the only cast-iron wave-swept lighthouse in the British Isles. Significantly the very first cast-iron lighthouse was not far away – on Swansea's west pier, having been designed by William Jernegan in 1803, and constructed with plates cast at Neath Abbey ironworks.

Materials were delivered to Whiteford by boat, but as the base is only exposed for between one and two hours at low tide, construction was extremely difficult. The lighthouse was built of eight cast-iron rings cast in Llanelli ironworks and bolted together externally. Whiteford lighthouse is 44ft high, and stands in 20ft of water at high tide. Access is by an external ladder (now removed) on the east side, leading to the balcony. A short ladder leads to a small upper balcony to enable the glass of the dome to be cleaned. From the main balcony a door leads into the lantern room, with an interior ladder to the store/living room. Although there was provision for two keepers, only one would have been in residence, alternating two weeks at Whiteford with two weeks at the Llanelli harbour lighthouse.

After 55 years service Whiteford lighthouse was de-commissioned in 1921, and replaced by a 12ft high light on Burry Holms, which was itself taken out of service in 1966.

For a few years from October 1982, Whiteford returned to use when an automatic light was installed to assist local sailors. Although Carmarthenshire County Council put the lighthouse up for sale for just £1, prospective buyers were deterred by the £100,000 cost of restoration. Hans Nicholas, in his survey of Whitford lighthouse commissioned by The Gower Society in 1998, described it as *"the only surviving wave-washed cast-iron lighthouse in Britain and one of only a handful in the world. Its survival must now be considered of international significance."* Yet even now the future of this Scheduled Ancient Monument is uncertain.

Pwll Du
(Harold Grenfell)

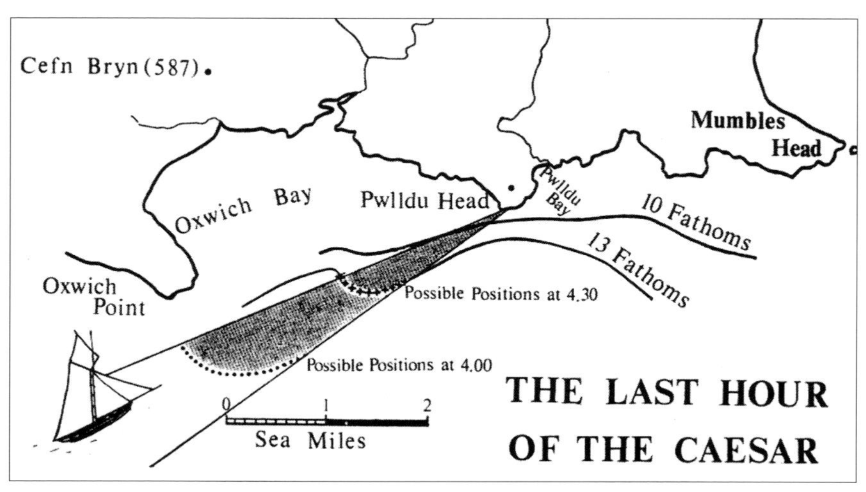

Caesar's route? (W. N. Jenkins, *Gower* XXVI, 1975)

THE WRECK OF THE *CAESAR*

Press gang tragedy

Press gang caricature 1780

Until 1814, when the Napoleonic wars ended, 'eligible men of seafaring habits between the ages of 18 and 45 years' risked being impressed into his Majesty's Navy during times of warfare. A walk from Caswell along the coastal path past Brandy Cove to the pebble-covered Pwll Du Bay brings us to the scene of a tragedy involving some men who had been forcibly enlisted into the Navy.

In 1760, during the Seven Years' War against France, a pressgang composed of twelve sailors under a Lieutenant from the Admiralty tender *Caesar* sought potential crewmen among the pubs around the Strand in Swansea. The *Caesar* was probably a requisitioned merchantman, which set sail on a spring tide from Swansea bound for Plymouth, carrying a number of impressed men. Stormy conditions in the Bristol Channel on 28th November caused the vessel to turn back, but in poor visibility the pilot mistook Pwll Du Head for Mumbles Head (this was thirty years before Mumbles lighthouse was built). The *Caesar* was holed on the rocks now named Caesar's Hole, and although the ship's master and mate escaped over the bowsprit before clambering onto High Pennard, they were apparently more interested in securing their own safety than in raising the alarm.

The next morning local people were aghast to find the wreck of the *Caesar*, and removed over sixty bodies. Most of these were the impressed men, who had been kept below deck (and possibly manacled), so had stood no chance of surviving once the ship was holed. Since many of these men had been impressed at Swansea, some of them may have been known to the local people.

Sixty-eight bodies were buried below Pwll Du Head in the area marked on Ordnance Survey maps as Graves End, where a circle of limestone rocks, visible when the undergrowth dies back, marks the burial site.

A British DUKW carrying US paratroopers across the River Waal, 30 September 1944
(Imperial War Museum)

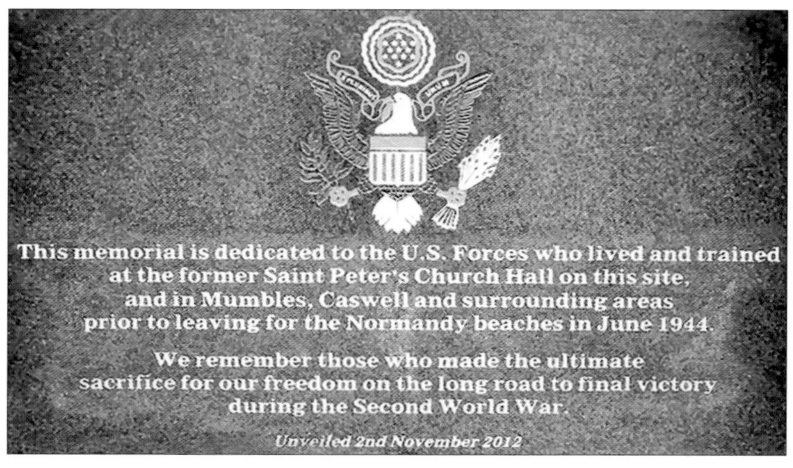

Newton's GIs memorial

YANKS IN MUMBLES

Remembering the D-Day heroes

The presence of American troops in Mumbles during the last war was remembered on 2nd November 2012, when a plaque was unveiled outside Newton Village Hall after a service at St Peter's church.

Newton Village Hall stands on the site of the church hall used by the Americans in preparation for the D-Day landings in northern France. The 2nd Infantry Division arrived in Swansea in April 1944, camping in the grounds of Oystermouth castle and in Singleton Park. Among the troops was future world heavyweight boxing champion Rocky Marciano.

Officers were housed in various places around the community, with the Officer's Mess in Summerland House. This stood near the top of Caswell Hill, behind Havergal Close, until demolished around 1995. US naval combat demolition units trained in Swansea Bay in clearing obstacles from the beaches, while Caswell, Oxwich, Port Eynon and Rhossili beaches were used for training for the Normandy landings.

Local people remember the troops having meals in Nissen Huts in Underhill Park. The Americans were popular with youngsters, dispensing packets of chewing gum in response to requests 'Got any gum, chum?' The Caswell valley provided good camouflage for jeeps, tanks and the DUKWs – the six-wheel-drive amphibious craft colloquially known as 'Ducks'. When the troops moved out for the D-Day landings, one 'Duck' was left behind and displayed outside Pressdee's garage in Mumbles. The community benefited from the surplus foodstuffs donated when the troops left.

'Omaha' was the code name for one of the Normandy beaches where the Allies landed on D-Day 6th June 1944 for the invasion of Europe. The original date chosen was 5th June, but the invasion was put back by 24 hours because of bad weather. Many of the troops who had trained in this area landed on Omaha beach and they suffered heavy casualties.

The Newton plaque states: 'This memorial is dedicated to the U.S. 2nd Infantry Division and other U.S. Forces who lived and trained in Caswell, and at the former St Peter's Church Hall on this site, before leaving for the Normandy beaches in June 1944.'

VERNON WATKINS by ALFRED JANES   Photograph by Tal Jones

GOWER

JOURNAL OF THE GOWER SOCIETY

VOLUME FIVE

Frontispiece to *Gower* V, 1953

"YOU TAUGHT US FIRST"

Film star inspires Gower poet

On Saturday afternoons during the First World War, in the days of silent films long before the advent of television, a bank manager's son would join excited youngsters outside the Uplands Cinema, waiting for the doors to open at 2 p.m. The cinema was on the site now occupied by Lloyds Bank, and the attraction was the serial starring Pearl White, where each episode ended with a 'cliff-hanger' which left the heroine in a desperately perilous situation, while the words 'to be continued next week' appeared on the screen.

Vernon Watkins, 1948

That boy was the future poet Vernon Watkins, whose father had moved from Maesteg to Eaton Crescent in the Uplands to manage Lloyds Bank in Wind Street (now the Revolution Bar). After the family settled at Redcliffe in Caswell (where the Redcliffe Apartments are now), Vernon went as a boarder to Repton School in Derbyshire. At Magdalene College,

Cambridge, he studied modern languages, but was dismayed at the analytical approach to literature, and left after a year. Following a nervous breakdown, he worked as a bank cashier at Lloyds in St Helen's Road (now William Hill's) so that he could live at home in Pennard, where his father had moved on retiring. That house, much enlarged, is now the Heatherslade Rest Home, where a plaque outside states that Vernon used to live there.

During the war Vernon worked in the government code-breaking centre at Bletchley Park, where he met his future wife Gwen. They lived at 'The Garth', a bungalow on Pennard cliffs above Heatherslade bay, while Vernon would travel by bus each day to work in St Helen's Road. A good friend and supporter of Dylan Thomas, Vernon's writing also appeared in print, starting with a book of poetry *Ballad of the Mari Llwyd* in 1941. After retiring from the bank, he died during a visit to Seattle aged 61, at a time when he was being considered among others as a possible Poet Laureate following John Masefield's death.

Inside Pennard church and on the cliffs above Deepslade are memorials to the poet of Gower, who was inspired to write of those boyhood visits to the Uplands Cinema in *Elegy on the Heroine of Childhood*, when he heard the news in 1938 of the death of Pearl White.

Four words catch hold. Dead exile, you would excite
In the red darkness, through the filtered light,
Our round, terrified eyes, when some
Demon of the rocks would come
And lock you in his house of moving walls:
You taught us first how loudly a pin falls.